BEATRIX POTTER BOOKS IN ORDER

ANTHONY MARKHAM

Contents

Beatrix Potter: A Biography

Helen Beatrix Potter was born on July 28, 1866, in Kensington, London, into a wealthy Unitarian family. Her father, Rupert Potter, was a barrister and amateur photographer, while her mother, Helen Leech Potter, was the daughter of a prosperous cotton merchant. The Potters, descendants of a line of Lancashire industrialists, enjoyed a life of privilege and comfort, residing in a large house in South Kensington, a rapidly developing area at the time.

Despite the family's wealth, the Potter household was somewhat austere and conventional. Beatrix and her younger brother, Bertram, were raised in an environment marked by strict Victorian values and a rigid social structure. Their childhood was largely spent indoors, under the watchful eye of governesses. This sheltered upbringing limited their interactions with other children, leading Beatrix and Bertram to find companionship and solace in their shared fascination with nature and the numerous pets they kept.

From a young age, Beatrix exhibited a keen interest in the natural world and a talent for drawing. She spent hours observing and sketching the flora and fauna around her, developing a meticulous eye for detail. The family's holidays in the countryside—particularly in Scotland and later in the Lake District—further nurtured her love of nature. These trips allowed Beatrix to explore the outdoors, where she collected specimens and filled her sketchbooks with drawings of plants, animals, and landscapes.

Beatrix's artistic talent was evident early on, and she received encouragement from her parents to develop her skills. Her father, an amateur photographer, provided her with access to his studio, where she honed her drawing and painting techniques. Despite the limitations placed on women during the Victorian era, Beatrix's parents supported her education in the arts, arranging for private lessons and encouraging her to study the works of renowned artists.

Beatrix's early life was also marked by her habit of keeping a journal. Between the ages of fourteen and thirty, she meticulously recorded her observations and thoughts in a series of notebooks. However, these were no ordinary diaries. Beatrix wrote in a tiny, secret code that she invented herself—a blend of letters, symbols, and mathematical symbols. This code was so complex that it remained undeciphered until 1958, when Leslie Linder, a collector of Potter's work, finally broke it.

The journals provide a fascinating glimpse into Beatrix's inner life and thoughts. They reveal her sharp intellect, her keen observational skills, and her often candid opinions about the people and events around her. Through her writings, we see a young woman who was intellectually curious and deeply engaged with the world, despite the constraints imposed by her Victorian upbringing.

Beatrix's transition from an amateur artist and diarist to a published author and illustrator began with a series of illustrated letters she wrote to the children of her former governess, Annie Moore. One such letter, written in 1893 to Annie's son Noel, featured a story about four little rabbits named Flopsy, Mopsy, Cottontail, and Peter. This letter, with its charming illustrations and engaging narrative, would later become the basis for "The Tale of Peter Rabbit."

Encouraged by the positive response from the Moore children and their mother, Beatrix decided to turn her illustrated letters into a book. However, her initial attempts to find a publisher were met with rejection. Determined, she decided to self-publish "The Tale of Peter Rabbit" in 1901. The first print run of 250 copies quickly sold out, catching the attention of the publishing house Frederick Warne & Co., who agreed to publish an enlarged edition in 1902. The book's success was immediate and phenomenal, leading to multiple reprints and establishing Beatrix Potter as a beloved children's author.

Following the success of "The Tale of Peter Rabbit," Beatrix continued to write and illustrate a series of children's books that would become classics. These included "The Tale of Squirrel Nutkin" (1903), "The Tailor of Gloucester" (1903), "The Tale of Benjamin Bunny" (1904), and "The Tale of Mrs. Tiggy-Winkle" (1905), among others. Her stories, characterized by their charming characters, engaging narratives, and exquisite illustrations, captivated young readers and remain popular to this day.

Beatrix's books were notable not only for their literary and artistic qualities but also for their innovative approach to children's literature. She insisted on small, affordable books that were easy for little hands to hold and read. She also believed in addressing her stories directly to children, which she felt was the secret to their success. Her attention to the practicalities of being an animal—whether it was a hedgehog's quills poking through a bonnet or a tortoise bringing a salad to a dinner party—added a unique charm and realism to her tales.

In addition to her literary achievements, Beatrix Potter was also a dedicated naturalist and scientist. Her keen interest in the natural world extended beyond her artistic pursuits to serious scientific study, particularly in the field of mycology, the study of fungi. She collected specimens, conducted experiments, and made detailed drawings of various fungi, which demonstrated her exceptional observational skills and scientific acumen.

In 1897, she wrote a paper titled "On the Germination of the Spores of Agaricineae," which presented her theories on the reproduction of fungi. Despite the quality of her research, Beatrix faced significant barriers as a woman in the male-dominated scientific community of her time. Her paper was presented to the Linnean Society of London by a male colleague, as women were not allowed to attend meetings or present their work. Although her contributions to mycology were not fully recognized during her lifetime, they have since been acknowledged as valuable to the field.

In her forties, Beatrix made a significant life change by purchasing Hill Top Farm in the village of Near Sawrey, in the Lake District, with the proceeds from her books. This move marked the beginning of a new chapter in her life, as she embraced the roles of farmer and conservationist. Hill Top became her sanctuary, a place where she could immerse herself in nature and draw inspiration for her work.

Beatrix's love for the Lake District went beyond mere appreciation; she was deeply committed to preserving its natural beauty and rural way of life. She acquired several farms and large tracts of land, which she managed with a keen eye for conservation and traditional farming practices. She became an expert in sheep breeding, particularly the local Herdwick breed, and won numerous prizes for her livestock.

Her work as a conservationist culminated in her partnership with the National Trust, an organization dedicated to preserving the natural and cultural heritage of the United Kingdom. Upon her death in 1943, Beatrix bequeathed her extensive land holdings—totaling over 4,000 acres—to the National Trust, ensuring that the landscapes she loved would be protected for future generations.

Beatrix Potter's personal life was marked by both joy and tragedy. In 1905, she became engaged to her publisher, Norman Warne. However, their happiness was short-lived, as Norman died of leukemia just a few weeks after their engagement. This devastating loss deeply affected Beatrix, but she found solace in her work and her growing connection to the Lake District.

In 1913, at the age of 47, Beatrix married William Heelis, a local solicitor who shared her love for the countryside and supported her conservation efforts. Their marriage was a happy and fulfilling partnership, and together they worked to protect and preserve the rural landscape they both cherished.

Beatrix Potter's legacy extends far beyond her beloved children's books. As an author and illustrator, she revolutionized children's literature with her unique blend of storytelling, artistry, and attention to detail. Her characters, such as Peter Rabbit, Jemima Puddle-Duck, and Mrs. Tiggy-Winkle, have become iconic figures, beloved by generations of readers.

Her contributions to natural science, particularly in the field of mycology, have also gained recognition over time. Her detailed illustrations and observations continue to be valued by scientists and historians alike.

Perhaps her greatest legacy is her work as a conservationist. Through her efforts to preserve the Lake District's natural beauty and traditional farming practices, Beatrix Potter played a crucial role in shaping the landscape as it exists today. The land she donated to the National Trust remains a testament to her commitment to conservation and her love for the countryside.

Beatrix Potter's life was a remarkable journey of creativity, resilience, and dedication. From her early years as a curious and observant child, through her success as a beloved children's author, to her later years as a passionate conservationist, she left an indelible mark on literature, science, and the natural world. Her legacy continues to inspire and enchant, reminding us of the enduring power of imagination and the importance of preserving our natural heritage.

Beatrix Potter Books In Order

Publication Order of Picture Books

The Tale of Peter Rabbit(1901)
The Tale of Squirrel Nutkin(1903)
The Tailor of Gloucester(1903)
The Tale of Benjamin Bunny(1904)
The Tale of Two Bad Mice(1904)
The Tale of Mrs. Tiggy-Winkle(1905)
The Tale of The Pie and The Patty-Pan(1905)
The Story of Miss Moppet(1906)
The Tale of Mr. Jeremy Fisher(1906)
The Story of A Fierce Bad Rabbit (1906)
The Tale of Tom Kitten(1907)
The Tale of Jemima Puddle-Duck (1908)
The Tale of Samuel Whiskers or the Roly-Poly Pudding (1908)
The Tale of the Flopsy Bunnies(1909)
The Tale of Ginger & Pickles (1909)

The Tale of Mrs. Tittlemouse (1910)
The Tale of Timmy Tiptoes (1911)
The Tale of Mr. Tod (1912)
The Tale of Pigling Bland (1913)
Appley Dapply's Nursery Rhymes (1917)
The Tale of Johnny Town-Mouse (1918)
Cecily Parsley's Nursery Rhymes (1922)
The Tale of Little Pig Robinson(1930)
The Fairy Caravan (1952)
The Tale of Kitty In Boots (2016)
The Christmas Present Hunt (2021)

Publication Order of Collections

Little Red Riding Hood: The Ultimate Collection (1697)
Peter Rabbit and Eleven Other Favorite Tales (1993)
Fairy Tales for Adults (2018)

Publication Order of Anthologies

Round the Christmas Tree (1983)
By a Woman's Hand (2010)
Animals We Love (2019)

Know Your Potter! A Ten Point Beatrix Potter Quiz

1. What name did Potter give to her first pet rabbit?

2. Who played the title role in the 2006 film Miss Potter?

3. In 1913 Potter married William Heelis, who had previously acted in what capacity?

4. In which Lakeland village is the visitor attraction The World of Beatrix Potter?

5. Peter Rabbit has three sisters, Flopsy, Mopsy and who else?

6. What is the name of the house in Cumbria, now owned by the National Trust, where Potter wrote many of her stories?

7. What type of animal is the title character in The Tale of Mr Tod?

8. Although she fell in love with the Lake District at an early age,
Potter was actually born in which city?

9. In The Tale of Squirrel Nutkin, which island do the squirrels visit?

10. In The Tale of Peter Rabbit, who owns the garden Peter invades?

Fifteen Things You Probably Didn't Know About Beatrix Potter

Even today, more than eighty years after her death, Beatrix Potter's beautifully illustrated tales—featuring animals and landscapes inspired by her beloved home in England's Lake District—remain incredibly popular. Here are 15 intriguing facts about the author of The Tale of Peter Rabbit:

1. Peter Rabbit wasn't an immediate success.

- Potter self-published The Tale of Peter Rabbit in 1901, funding a print run of 250 herself after being turned down by several publishers. In 1902, the book was republished by Frederick Warne & Co after Potter agreed to redo her black-and-white illustrations in colour. By the end of its first year, it was reprinted six times due to high demand.

2. Beatrix Potter asked that one of her books not be published in England.

- In 1926, Potter published The Fairy Caravan, which was initially released only in America as she felt it was too autobiographical for

England. She also believed it wasn't as good as her other works. The book was finally released in the UK nine years after her death.

3. Beatrix Potter's later books had to be cobbled together from early drawings.

- As her eyesight diminished, it became harder for Potter to produce her signature illustrations. Consequently, many of her later books were pieced together from earlier drawings in her extensive sketchbooks. The Tale of Little Pig Robinson, published in 1930, was her last picture book.

4. Beatrix Potter sometimes wrote in secret code.

- Between 1881 and 1897, Potter kept a journal in which she jotted down her private thoughts in a secret code. This code was so complex it was not deciphered until 1958.

5. A lost work of Beatrix Potter's was published in 2016.

- A lost Potter story, The Tale of Kitty-in-Boots, was rediscovered in 2013 and published in 2016. Publisher Jo Hanks found references to the story in an out-of-print biography and searched the Victoria and Albert Museum archive, finding a sketch and a rough manuscript. Quentin Blake provided supplementary illustrations for the publication.

6. Beatrix Potter wrote prolifically.

- Potter was a prolific writer, producing 28 books, including The Tale of Squirrel Nutkin, The Tale of Mrs Tiggy Winkle, and The Tale of Mr. Jeremy Fisher. Her stories have been translated into 35 languages and sold over 100 million copies.

7. Beatrix Potter understood the power of merchandising.

- In 1903, recognising the merchandising potential, Potter made her own Peter Rabbit doll, which she registered at the Patent Office. A Peter Rabbit board game and wallpaper were also produced during her lifetime.

8. Beatrix wasn't Potter's real first name.

- Beatrix Potter was born in London on 28 July 1866 and was christened Helen after her mother. She was known by her more distinctive middle name: Beatrix.

9. Beatrix Potter was a naturalist at a time when most women weren't.

- Potter was fascinated by nature and constantly recorded the world around her in her drawings. She became an accomplished scientific illustrator, particularly interested in fungi. She wrote a paper, "On the Germination of the Spores of Agaricineae," proposing her theory on fungi spore reproduction. The paper was presented on her behalf by the

Assistant Director of Kew Gardens to the Linnean Society on 1 April 1897, as women were not allowed to attend the meetings.

10. Peter Rabbit and his friends were partly based on Beatrix Potter's own pets.

- Peter was modelled on Potter's pet rabbit, Peter Piper—a cherished bunny she frequently sketched and took for walks on a leash. Her first pet rabbit, Benjamin Bouncer, inspired Benjamin Bunny, Peter's cousin. Potter loved sketching Benjamin, too. After a publisher purchased some of her sketches of Benjamin in 1890, she rewarded him with hemp seeds, which made him "intoxicated and wholly unmanageable" the next morning, as she noted in her diary.

11. Beatrix Potter was an accomplished sheep farmer.

- Potter was an award-winning sheep farmer and the first woman elected President of the Herdwick Sheep Breeders' Association in 1943.

12. The Tale of Peter Rabbit was inspired by a letter.

- Potter's most famous book, The Tale of Peter Rabbit, was inspired by an illustrated letter she wrote to Noel, the son of her former governess, Annie, in 1893. She later borrowed the letter back, copied the pictures and story, and adapted it into the beloved tale.

13. You can visit Hill Top, Beatrix Potter's home.

- Upon her death in 1943 at 77, Potter left 14 farms and 4,000 acres in the Lake District to the National Trust, preserving the landscape that inspired her work. The Trust opened her house, Hill Top, to the public in 1946.

14. Beatrix Potter's house was essentially a menagerie.

- Potter kept numerous pets in her schoolroom at home—rabbits, hedgehogs, frogs, and mice. She would capture wild mice and let them run loose, shaking a handkerchief to recapture them. When her brother Bertram went to boarding school, he left behind a pair of long-eared pet bats. One was set free, but the other, a rarer specimen, she euthanised with chloroform and stuffed for her collection.

15. Beatrix Potter was reportedly a disappointment to her mum.

- Despite her success, Potter disappointed her mother, who wanted her to make an advantageous marriage and accompany her on social calls. In 1905, Potter accepted a proposal from her publisher Norman Warne, but her parents disapproved, deeming him unsuitable. Warne died of leukaemia weeks after the engagement. Potter eventually married at 47 to solicitor William Heelis.

About Hill Top

Immerse yourself in the world of Beatrix Potter by visiting Hill Top, her beloved home that sparked her creativity and passion for the Lake District.

The garden in the summertime at Hill Top, Cumbria

Explore the charming cottage garden, a picturesque blend of flowers, herbs, fruits, and vegetables. Wander along the garden path to the front door and see firsthand why Beatrix held this place so dear. Acquired in 1905 with the proceeds from her first book, The Tale of Peter Rabbit, Hill Top and its surrounding countryside inspired many of her subsequent stories.

The Parlour at Hill Top, Sawrey, Cumbria, with an Adam style fireplace

The entrance hall at Hill Top, home of Beatrix Potter, in Cumbria

Now a treasured National Trust property, Hill Top offers visitors a glimpse into Beatrix Potter's life and legacy. To visit, head towards Hawkshead in Cumbria. From there, follow signs to Near Sawrey, where Hill Top is located. The journey through the scenic Lake District is an experience in itself, setting the perfect stage for your visit to this historic home.

The Secret Life of Beatrix Potter

Beatrix Potter, a British author and illustrator, is renowned for her children's books, including "The Tale of Peter Rabbit." Born in London in 1866, Potter felt a profound connection to the countryside, which profoundly influenced her work.

Many teenagers go to great lengths to keep their diaries private, but Beatrix Potter took this to an extreme. Between the ages of fourteen and thirty, she meticulously recorded her observations of the rigid Victorian society in several journals. Born to wealthy and proper parents, descendants of Northern England's cotton merchants, Potter perhaps felt the need to protect her thoughts. She wrote in minuscule handwriting using a complex code that remained undeciphered until 1958 when a collector, through a reference to Louis XVI, painstakingly decoded years of Potter's innermost musings.

In public, Potter, the creator of "The Tale of Peter Rabbit" and "The Tale of Benjamin Bunny," appeared demure and respectable. However, her journals reveal a different side: forthright, opinionated, and an artist who revelled in the details and humour of everyday life. Living in a grand South Kensington house until she was forty-seven, Potter often felt like an outsider. She loathed the city's noise and grime, longing for nature, and referred to her birthplace as "unloved."

During her childhood, Potter seldom ventured into London and had few friends aside from her younger brother, Bertram. She spent her days drawing compulsively, using a sketchbook made from drawer-lining paper and stationery. Drawing was her solace, regardless of the subject matter.

In her forties, Potter made a dramatic shift. She abandoned the trappings of her privileged London life and bought a cottage in the remote English countryside. She became a farmer and conservationist, embracing a life of muddy shoes and prize-winning sheep. She roamed the fells and lakeside paths around her new home, sketching the landscapes and ultimately preserving them from destruction.

Potter may have had few friends as a child, but she was never without animals. She and Bertram smuggled various pets into their nursery, including snakes, salamanders, lizards, rabbits, frogs, and a hedgehog.

In her early adulthood, Potter closely observed her pets, crafting narratives about them and filling her letters to friends' children with their adventures. Her playful and vivid letters, illustrated with pen-and-ink drawings, were lively tales of rabbit escapades. In 1892, she wrote a letter to Noel Moore, the son of her former governess, recounting Benjamin Bunny's encounter with a wild rabbit. After Benjamin's death, Peter Piper became her muse. In 1893, she wrote to Noel again: "My dear Noel, I don't know what to write to you, so I shall tell you a story about four little rabbits whose names were Flopsy, Mopsy, Cottontail and Peter." Her illustration of Peter on his hind legs, ears perked, instantly suggested mischief.

Potter's letters to the Moore children were so cherished that Noel's mother suggested she turn them into books. In 1901, Potter self-published "The Tale of Peter Rabbit," mirroring the story she had written to Noel, complete with Peter's "blue jacket with brass buttons, quite new." After multiple rejections from established publishers who balked at her insistence on an affordable price and small size for children's hands, Frederick Warne & Co. agreed to publish an abridged version. Potter reluctantly accepted their chosen cover image, describing it as an "idiotic prancing rabbit."

"Peter Rabbit" became an instant success, selling out multiple editions. "The public must be fond of rabbits! what an appalling quantity of Peter," Potter remarked. Her publisher demanded more, leading her to create a string of beloved books, starting with "The Tale of Squirrel Nutkin" and "The Tailor of Gloucester." She even patented her characters.

Potter believed her books resonated because they were written for real children. "It is much more satisfactory to address a real live child," she wrote. "I often think that that was the secret of the success of Peter Rabbit, it was written to a child—not made to order."

Her knack for blending the familiar with the strange made her stories captivating. Her attention to the practicalities of animal life produced enchanting images. In "The Tale of Mrs. Tiggy-Winkle," a hedgehog's quills poke through her bonnet. In "The Tale of Mr. Jeremy Fisher," a tortoise invited to dinner brings a salad in a string bag. Potter took silliness seriously, crafting whimsical yet relatable tales that continue to delight readers today.

Quiz Answers

QUESTION ONE
Peter. She also used the name in her 1904 sequel to the 1902 book, The Tale of Peter Rabbit - The Tale of Benjamin Bunny.

QUESTION TWO
The correct answer is Renee Zellweger. The film has many inaccuracies. One sequence portrays The Tale of Jemima Puddleduck as one of the early publications. It was in fact published in 1908, after the period shown in the film ends

QUESTION THREE
The correct answer is Her solicitor. William and Beatrix were married in October 1913, when Beatrix was 47

QUESTION FOUR
The correct answer is Bowness. The Attraction is in Bowness-on-Windermere, a scenic town with views of the lake and mountains.

QUESTION FIVE
The correct answer is Cotton-tail. Peter also has a cousin, Benjamin Bunny.

QUESTION SIX
It's Hill-Top. It's near the village of Sawrey in The Lake District.

QUESTION SEVEN

It's a fox. He has a squabble with Tommy Brock the badger.

QUESTION EIGHT
She was born in Kensington, London, and was the daughter of a barrister.

QUESTION NINE

It was Owl Island. The squirrels visit Old Brown's island six times. On each visit, Nutkin taunts Old Brown with a riddle. At the end of the story, Nutkin is caught and punished.

QUESTION TEN
The correct answer is Mr McGregor. Mr McGregor appears in three stories, The Tale of Peter Rabbit, The Tale of Benjamin Bunny and The Tale of the Flopsy Bunnies.